In This New Place
Poems

by Linda Marino

Illustrated by Rosario Valderrama

PEARSON

Glenview, Illinois • Boston, Massachusetts • Chandler, Arizona
Upper Saddle River, New Jersey

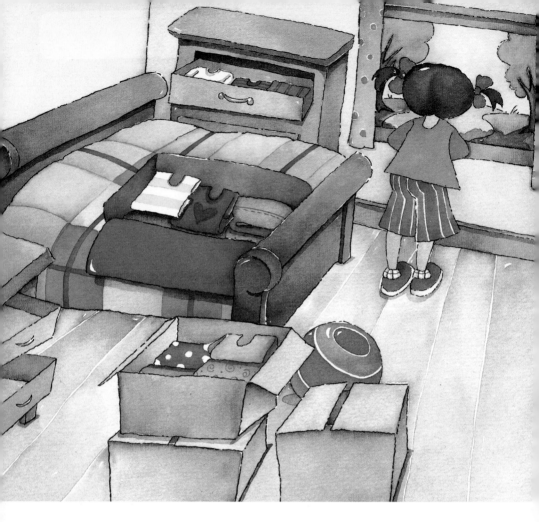

Questions

Who is in my old room
Where I used to watch the sky?
Who sees the changes on the street
As the day goes by?

What is in my room today,
In that place I used to play?
Is there still a part of me
Looking out the window at a tree?

Where Am I From?

Where am I from?
I am from a country far away.
I want to be like the other kids.
They say things I do not understand.
I try to talk like them,
But they sound so different!

I look in the mirror.
Where am I from?
I miss my home.
I miss my country.
I miss the songs I used to hear.
I think of the voices of the people here.
I miss the voices of my home.

In This New Place

In this new place
I must admit
I miss the place
Where I used to fit.

In this new place
I will go to class,
Make new friends,
And let time pass.

In this new place,
In this new time,
It is not perfect,
But it is mine.

pizza

BLT sandwich

First Time in the Cafeteria

"Pizza" I know. They serve it every day.
But a hero sandwich?
What is that?
Is it a tiny man wearing a cape?
Does he push through lettuce
To meet us?
What fun that would be!

I wonder—what is a BLT?
Do you have to be in a club
To eat a club sandwich?
Soon I will know what it all means.
Right now I am not sure what to do.
I could eat pizza today.
But no! I will try new things!
I would like a hero, please!

People live in different parts of the United States. They use different words for the same thing. For example:

A hero sandwich has meat and cheese. It has pickles and other things too.

In Philadelphia, this sandwich is called a *hoagie*. In the Northeast, it is a *grinder* or a *sub*. In the South, it is a *poor boy*. It has other names in other places too.

hero sandwich

Supply List for a New Student

One new lock,
Five blue pens—
A bit of courage
To make new friends.
A ruler with inches
And other marks too—
Knowing who you are
And all that you can do.
Plenty of pencils,
Notebooks for each class—
A good supply of hope
That lonely times will pass.

lock

notebooks

ruler